Genre-Specific Conflict & Tension Guide

Crafting High-Stakes Stories for Every Genre

Connie Bauldree
Author by Design

Genre-Specific Conflict & Tension Guide: Crafting High-Stakes Stories for Every Genre

Published by BaulConn Publishing www.authorbydesign.co www.writersblockboxes.com

Introduction

Conflict and tension might be universal, but every genre has its own flavor, and its own reader expectations. What feels like high-stakes drama in a romance might fall flat in a thriller, and the tension that works in horror won't always translate to contemporary fiction.

This guide is your shortcut to mastering conflict and tension, no matter what you write. Inside, you'll find:

- The classic conflicts and tension sources that define each genre
- Practical tips for raising stakes and keeping readers on edge
- Common pitfalls to avoid (so your story never feels generic)
- Quick prompts and brainstorming ideas to spark new twists
- Exercises to help you tailor your story's conflict and tension for maximum impact

Whether you're plotting a slow-burn romance, a twisty thriller, or a sweeping fantasy, you'll find genre-specific advice, examples, and hands-on tools to make your story unputdownable.

Pro Tip: *Don't be afraid to blend genres or borrow techniques! The best stories often surprise readers by twisting expectations and raising the stakes in fresh ways.*

Ready to dive in? Let's start with Romance and build your story's conflict and tension, one genre at a time.

Romance

What Readers Expect:

Romance thrives on emotional tension, longing, and obstacles that keep lovers apart. Readers want to feel the push-pull of desire, uncertainty, and risk - right up to the final page.

Classic Conflicts & Tension Sources:

- Misunderstandings and secrets
- Competing goals or values
- External forces (family, society, distance)
- Past heartbreak or trust issues
- The "will they/won't they" slow burn

Tips for Raising Stakes:

- Make the cost of love personal (risking vulnerability, reputation, or cherished dreams)
- Use near-misses and almost-confessions to stretch out tension
- Let characters make mistakes, then force them to fight for a second chance

Common Pitfalls:

- Resolving the main conflict too soon (no tension left for Act 3)
- Mistaking drama for conflict: manufactured arguments that don't grow from character
- Characters who don't have enough at stake (make us care what they risk losing!)

Quick Prompts & Twists:

- What secret, if revealed, would threaten the relationship?
- How does one character's goal clash with the other's?
- Who or what is standing in the way? Family, friends, distance, or a belief?

- What's the moment when both characters almost walk away?

Exercise:

Write a one-paragraph summary of your romance's central conflict. Then list three ways you could make the stakes more personal or the obstacles harder to overcome.

Mystery/Thriller

What Readers Expect:

Mystery and thriller readers crave suspense, danger, and a steady drip of secrets. Every clue, red herring, and twist should raise new questions and tighten the screws on your protagonist.

Classic Conflicts & Tension Sources:

- The pursuit of truth versus personal safety or loyalty
- Cat-and-mouse games between protagonist and antagonist
- Time pressure: racing against a deadline, ticking clocks
- Unreliable allies, hidden motives, or betrayals
- The cost of uncovering secrets. What's at risk if the truth comes out?

Tips for Raising Stakes:

- Make every clue matter. Each discovery should complicate the case or deepen the danger
- Use unreliable narrators, shifting alliances, or ambiguous evidence
- Let your protagonist risk not just their life, but their reputation, relationships, or sanity

Common Pitfalls:

- Withholding too much information. Confusing readers rather than intriguing them
- Coincidence-driven twists that don't grow from character choices
- Flat antagonists. Make sure the villain's motives and stakes are as strong as the hero's

Quick Prompts & Twists:

- What's the one clue your protagonist missed and what are the consequences?

- Who benefits most if the truth stays hidden?
- How does a personal connection to the case complicate your protagonist's choices?
- What's the "point of no return," where solving the mystery becomes truly dangerous?

Exercise:

Write a one-paragraph summary of your story's core mystery or threat. Then list three ways you could make the investigation more personal, urgent, or risky for your protagonist.

Horror

What Readers Expect:

Horror readers want to feel unsettled, vulnerable, and exposed to the unknown. The best horror stories build dread, escalate danger, and force characters to confront both external terrors and their own inner demons.

Classic Conflicts & Tension Sources:

- Survival: character vs. monster, supernatural force, or human evil
- Isolation: cut off from help, no one believes them, trapped
- Unreliable senses or reality: hallucinations, dreams, or gaslighting
- Secrets and forbidden knowledge; what's hidden should terrify
- Fear of corruption: being changed, possessed, or "becoming the monster"

Tips for Raising Stakes:

- Use atmosphere and setting to amplify unease (weather, darkness, silence, claustrophobia)
- Escalate the threat: let characters believe they're safe, then pull the rug out
- Mix external horror (monsters, threats) with internal horror (guilt, shame, fear)

Common Pitfalls:

- Relying on gore or jump scares instead of building psychological dread
- Making characters act irrationally just to move the plot
- Resolving horror too neatly. Sometimes the best endings leave questions or lingering dread

Quick Prompts & Twists:

- What's the one thing your character is most afraid of? How can you force them to face it?
- Who (or what) can't be trusted?
- How does isolation, (physical or emotional), raise the stakes?
- What secret, if revealed, would destroy hope or sanity?

Exercise:

Describe your story's central horror or threat in one paragraph. Then list three ways you could increase dread, escalate danger, or blur the line between reality and fear.

Fantasy

What Readers Expect:

Fantasy readers crave epic stakes, magical systems, and worlds where conflict can shape destinies. The best fantasy stories weave personal struggles with sweeping external forces (magic, prophecy, war, or ancient secrets).

Classic Conflicts & Tension Sources:

- Power struggles: rival kingdoms, magical orders, or family legacies
- The burden (and cost) of prophecy or destiny
- Conflicts over magic. Who wields it, who's forbidden, what's the price?
- "Fish out of water" tension: characters thrust into unfamiliar worlds
- Loyalty vs. ambition: torn between duty and desire

Tips for Raising Stakes:

- Tie world-scale conflict to your protagonist's personal journey
- Escalate by forcing hard choices between love, loyalty, and survival
- Use magical rules and limitations to complicate plans and create setbacks

Common Pitfalls:

- Overloading with lore or backstory at the expense of present conflict
- Making magic a "fix-all" instead of a source of new problems
- Villains who want power "just because". Give them real motives

Quick Prompts & Twists:

- What's one magical rule or limitation that creates unexpected conflict?
- How does prophecy (true or not) force your character into action or doubt?
- Who stands to lose the most if the balance of power shifts?
- What's the cost of using magic? Emotionally, physically, or morally?

Exercise:

Summarize your fantasy story's core conflict in one paragraph. Then list three ways magic, prophecy, or world politics could raise the stakes or complicate your protagonist's journey.

Science Fiction

What Readers Expect:

Sci-fi readers want to see how technology, discovery, and the unknown shape conflict and tension. The best sci-fi stories pit characters against shifting realities, ethical dilemmas, and forces far bigger than themselves.

Classic Conflicts & Tension Sources:

- Man vs. technology: AI, surveillance, or inventions gone wrong
- Survival in hostile environments (space, alien worlds, dystopias)
- Ethical dilemmas: progress vs. humanity, freedom vs. control
- First contact or the threat of the unknown
- Power struggles: corporations, governments, rebels, or outcasts

Tips for Raising Stakes:

- Make technology or discovery both a tool and a threat. What's gained, what's lost?
- Escalate by revealing hidden motives or unintended consequences
- Let characters face impossible choices with no easy answers

Common Pitfalls:

- Info-dumping technical details instead of showing conflict through action
- Solutions that are too convenient ("tech saves the day" with no cost)
- Focusing on big ideas but neglecting personal stakes

Quick Prompts & Twists:

- What's one unintended consequence of a new technology?
- Who is watching, controlling, or manipulating your protagonist?
- How does the environment (space, future Earth, virtual worlds) add danger?
- What's the ethical line your character might cross and what's the fallout?

Exercise:

Write a one-paragraph summary of your sci-fi story's central conflict. Then list three ways technology, discovery, or the unknown could escalate tension or force tough decisions.

Historical Fiction

What Readers Expect:

Historical fiction readers want to be immersed in another era, feeling the weight of real-world events, customs, and constraints. The most compelling stories blend personal conflict with the pressures of time, place, and society.

Classic Conflicts & Tension Sources:

- Duty vs. desire: personal dreams at odds with family, tradition, or societal norms
- War, revolution, or disaster as external forces shaping personal stakes
- Secrets, scandals, or forbidden relationships in a rigid society
- Survival amid historical upheaval (plague, famine, persecution)
- The cost of progress or change (old ways vs. new)

Tips for Raising Stakes:

- Tie your protagonist's journey to real historical events or turning points
- Escalate by making personal choices carry public or generational consequences
- Let historical constraints (laws, gender roles, class) be active obstacles

Common Pitfalls:

- Overloading with research or period detail at the expense of story momentum
- Characters with modern attitudes that don't fit the era
- Reluctance to show the true hardship or danger of the time

Quick Prompts & Twists:

- What's one rule or expectation your protagonist is tempted to break?
- How does a public event (war, trial, scandal) upend private lives?
- Who risks everything to protect a secret and what's the fallout?
- How does the past haunt or shape your characters?

Exercise:

Summarize your historical fiction's core conflict in one paragraph. Then list three ways the setting's constraints or upheavals could raise the stakes or complicate your protagonist's choices.

Contemporary/Literary

What Readers Expect:
Contemporary and literary fiction readers crave authentic, character-driven conflict and nuanced tension. These stories often explore identity, relationships, and the quiet struggles beneath everyday life.

Classic Conflicts & Tension Sources:
- Family dynamics, generational clashes, or old wounds resurfacing
- Identity, belonging, and the search for meaning or purpose
- Secrets, betrayals, or unspoken resentments among friends or lovers
- Social pressures: fitting in, standing out, or breaking free
- The tension of ordinary moments. What's left unsaid, what's just out of reach

Tips for Raising Stakes:
- Make small moments matter. Show how a single conversation or decision can change everything
- Escalate through emotional honesty, vulnerability, or risk-taking
- Layer tension through subtext, silence, and what's not resolved

Common Pitfalls:
- Scenes that meander without clear stakes or direction
- Characters who are passive or don't want anything deeply enough
- Relying on coincidence or melodrama instead of earned conflict

Quick Prompts & Twists:

- What's a truth your character is afraid to admit to themselves or others?
- How does a minor misunderstanding spiral into a major rift?
- Who holds the power in a relationship, and how does it shift?
- What's a small risk that feels huge to your protagonist?

Exercise:

Write a one-paragraph summary of your story's central emotional conflict. Then list three ways you could add tension through subtext, silence, or shifting power dynamics.

Young Adult (YA)

What Readers Expect:

YA readers crave fast-paced stories with high emotional stakes, identity struggles, and the intensity of first experiences. Conflict often centers on coming of age, self-discovery, and finding one's place in a world that doesn't always understand.

Classic Conflicts & Tension Sources:

- Identity vs. expectation: fitting in, rebelling, or forging a new path
- Friendships tested by secrets, jealousy, or betrayal
- Family conflict (generational clashes, independence vs. protection)
- First love, heartbreak, or unrequited feelings
- Facing authority figures, rules, or societal pressures

Tips for Raising Stakes:

- Make consequences feel immediate and life-changing (even if the scope is personal)
- Escalate through misunderstandings, shifting alliances, or peer pressure
- Let characters make mistakes and learn from them. Growth is part of the journey

Common Pitfalls:

- Adults solving problems for teen characters
- Overly mature or unrealistic dialogue/behavior
- Conflict that feels trivial or manufactured. Make it matter to your protagonist

Quick Prompts & Twists:

- What's one secret that could ruin a friendship or romance?
- How does your protagonist's greatest fear get

tested?

- Who must choose between loyalty to friends and doing what's right?
- What's the risk of telling the truth or keeping it hidden?

Exercise:

Summarize your YA story's central conflict in one paragraph. Then list three ways you could raise the stakes for your protagonist's identity, relationships, or future.

Women's Fiction

What Readers Expect:

Women's fiction explores the complexities of identity, family, friendship, and personal growth, often with layered conflicts that span relationships, careers, and self-worth. Readers want emotional honesty, resilience, and the tension between individual needs and external expectations.

Classic Conflicts & Tension Sources:

- Balancing personal dreams with family or societal roles
- Friendships tested by secrets, change, or time
- Marital or romantic tension (infidelity, trust, new beginnings)
- Generational conflict: mothers/daughters, tradition vs. change
- Navigating loss, reinvention, or second chances

Tips for Raising Stakes:

- Make internal conflict as urgent as external. What's the cost of choosing self over others?
- Escalate by forcing tough choices and moral dilemmas
- Layer tension through shifting relationships, betrayals, or unexpected support

Common Pitfalls:

- Resolving conflict too easily or neatly. Let things get messy
- Focusing only on romance. Show the full spectrum of a character's life
- Stereotypes or "cookie-cutter" struggles. Make conflicts specific and personal

Quick Prompts & Twists:

- What's the one thing your protagonist can't say out loud?
- How does a family secret or past mistake resurface at the worst time?
- Who must choose between loyalty and personal happiness?
- What's the risk of starting over—and what's the cost of staying the same?

Exercise:
Describe your women's fiction story's central dilemma in one paragraph. Then list three ways you could intensify the conflict through relationships, secrets, or personal stakes.

Paranormal/Urban Fantasy

What Readers Expect:

Paranormal and urban fantasy readers want the real world with a twist - magic, monsters, and mysteries lurking beneath the surface. The best stories blend supernatural conflict with personal stakes, keeping tension high both in the streets and in the heart.

Classic Conflicts & Tension Sources:

- Hidden worlds: characters caught between everyday life and the supernatural
- Power struggles: rival magical factions, ancient feuds, or forbidden knowledge
- The cost of magic: using powers comes with risks, rules, or sacrifices
- Identity conflict: what it means to be "other," hiding true nature, or choosing between worlds
- Human vs. supernatural: romance, rivalry, or uneasy alliances

Tips for Raising Stakes:

- Escalate by making the supernatural threat more personal or impossible to ignore
- Layer tension: the danger of discovery, the pull between loyalty and survival, or the risk of losing one's humanity
- Use magic or paranormal abilities to complicate relationships, not just solve problems

Common Pitfalls:

- Overpowered characters with no real obstacles
- Relying on genre tropes (vampires, werewolves, secret societies) without fresh twists
- Neglecting the "real world" stakes. Make sure characters have something to lose in both

worlds

Quick Prompts & Twists:

- What's the one rule of magic or the supernatural that your protagonist is tempted to break?
- Who is watching, hunting, or manipulating from the shadows?
- How does hiding a secret identity strain relationships or create danger?
- What's the cost of embracing (or rejecting) supernatural power?

Exercise:

Write a one-paragraph summary of your story's supernatural conflict. Then list three ways you could raise the stakes by tying the paranormal threat to your protagonist's personal life, relationships, or identity.

Blending Genres & Twisting Expectations

Why Blend Genres?

Some of the most memorable stories break the rules - combining genres, subverting tropes, and delivering conflict and tension that readers haven't seen before. Blending genres lets you raise the stakes, add fresh twists, and keep your story unpredictable.

Classic Blends & Their Unique Conflicts:

- **Romantic Thriller:** Love and danger collide. Can you trust the person you're falling for?
- **Historical Fantasy:** Magic in the past. What happens when old world rules meet new world power?
- **Science Fiction Mystery:** The search for truth in a world shaped by technology and secrets
- **Paranormal Romance:** The risks (and rewards) of loving across worlds or species
- **Contemporary Horror:** Everyday life invaded by the uncanny or terrifying

Tips for Raising Tension in Blended Genres:

- Use the expectations of one genre to set up a twist, then flip the script with a surprise from the other
- Let conflicts from each genre collide or compound (e.g., a magical secret threatens a political alliance)
- Make sure the stakes matter in both genres (personal and world-shaking, emotional and external)
- Don't be afraid to break "the rules", but know what they are first, so you can subvert them with purpose

Common Pitfalls:

- Trying to juggle too many genre conventions. Focus on the core conflicts and stakes
- Neglecting character motivation in favor of plot twists
- Letting one genre overpower the other. Balance is key

Quick Prompts & Twists:

- What's a trope from one genre you can twist with a rule from another? (e.g., a "chosen one" who doesn't want the job, a detective who discovers magic is real)
- How do the rules of each genre clash or create new problems?
- Who is caught between worlds, loyalties, or identities?
- What's the risk of breaking convention and what's the reward?

Exercise:

Describe your blended genre story in one paragraph.

Then list three ways you could twist reader expectations, raise the stakes, or create unique sources of conflict and tension by blending genres.

Conflict & Tension Checklists

Romance

- ☐ Do my main characters have clear, opposing goals or secrets?
- ☐ Are the stakes personal and emotional for both lovers?
- ☐ Is there a believable obstacle keeping them apart?
- ☐ Does tension escalate through misunderstandings, near-misses, or risk?
- ☐ Is the resolution earned (not just a convenient "happily ever after")?

Mystery/Thriller

- ☐ Is there a central mystery or threat driving the story?
- ☐ Does each clue or twist raise new questions or dangers?
- ☐ Are both protagonist and antagonist's motives strong and clear?
- ☐ Is there a ticking clock or urgent deadline?
- ☐ Do personal stakes complicate the investigation?

Horror

- ☐ Does dread or danger escalate throughout the story?
- ☐ Are both external threats and inner fears present?
- ☐ Is the atmosphere (setting, weather, isolation) used to build tension?
- ☐ Do characters make choices that worsen their situation?
- ☐ Is there a lingering sense of unease, even after the climax?

Fantasy

- ☐ Are world-scale conflicts tied to personal stakes?
- ☐ Do magical rules or limitations create problems, not just solutions?
- ☐ Are power struggles and loyalties tested?
- ☐ Is prophecy or destiny a source of conflict, not just a plot device?
- ☐ Are villains' motives as strong as the hero's?

Science Fiction

- ☐ Does technology or discovery create both opportunity and threat?
- ☐ Are ethical dilemmas and unintended consequences explored?
- ☐ Is the environment (space, dystopia, virtual world) a source of danger?
- ☐ Do characters face impossible choices with real fallout?
- ☐ Are personal stakes as strong as the "big idea"?

Historical Fiction

- ☐ Are personal conflicts shaped by real historical events or pressures?
- ☐ Do societal rules or expectations act as active obstacles?
- ☐ Are secrets, scandals, or forbidden relationships present?
- ☐ Does the setting influence every major choice?
- ☐ Are consequences public as well as private?

Contemporary/Literary

- ☐ Does every scene have emotional or relational stakes?
- ☐ Are conflicts layered (internal, interpersonal, societal)?
- ☐ Is subtext, silence, or power dynamic used to add tension?
- ☐ Do small moments have big impact?
- ☐ Is the resolution honest, not just tidy?

Young Adult

- ☐ Are identity, belonging, and independence at the heart of the conflict?
- ☐ Do friendships and first loves face real tests?
- ☐ Are consequences immediate and life-changing (to the protagonist)?
- ☐ Are characters allowed to make mistakes and grow?
- ☐ Is adult intervention minimized?

Women's Fiction

- ☐ Are characters balancing personal dreams with external roles?
- ☐ Are friendships, family, and romance tested by secrets or change?
- ☐ Are internal dilemmas as urgent as external ones?
- ☐ Do relationships shift, evolve, or break under pressure?
- ☐ Is the ending emotionally honest, even if messy?

Paranormal/Urban Fantasy

- ☐ Are supernatural conflicts tied to real-world stakes?
- ☐ Does the cost of magic or power escalate?
- ☐ Are hidden worlds or identities a source of tension?
- ☐ Do human and supernatural problems collide?
- ☐ Are genre tropes twisted or made fresh?

Blended Genres

- ☐ Do conflicts from each genre intersect or compound?
- ☐ Are reader expectations set up and then twisted?
- ☐ Is the balance between genres maintained throughout?
- ☐ Are stakes high in both genres (personal and world-shaking)?
- ☐ Does the story surprise, challenge, or subvert the "rules" in satisfying ways?

Conflict and tension are the heartbeat of every unforgettable story, no matter the genre. You now have the tools, prompts, and checklists to craft high-stakes fiction that keeps readers turning pages.

Remember:

- Raise the stakes, complicate the journey, and never make it too easy for your characters.
- Trust your instincts. If you feel the tension, your readers will too.
- Don't be afraid to break the rules or blend genres. The best stories surprise even their authors.

Keep this guide handy as you draft, revise, and brainstorm. And if you ever get stuck, revisit the exercises, templates, and checklists. You're never more than a twist away from something brilliant.

About The Author

Connie Bauldree is a self-published author with a passion for storytelling and helping others craft their own. Writing under the pen names Connie Connolly, Emersyn Kane, Payton Rome, and Connie Bauldree, she has authored over 75 non-fiction writing resources and published nine fiction novels spanning multiple genres.

Connie is the owner of Author by Design, the creative hub behind the Builder Series and the Writer's Block Box, resources designed to inspire and empower writers at every stage of their journey. She is also the co-founder of SisterScribe Academy, a platform dedicated to supporting and educating aspiring authors.

Connie believes every writer has a story worth telling and is passionate about providing the tools and frameworks to help them succeed.

When she's not writing or developing innovative tools for authors, Connie enjoys connecting with her audience on social media. Follow her @authorbydesign for tips, updates, and inspiration.

Stay in touch and explore her offerings by signing up for her newsletter at www.authorbydesign.co. or www.writersblockboxes.com.